Strategies for Networking

ISBN-13:
978-1514238639

ISBN-10:
1514238632

Defining the Art of Networking

Networking is defined in many terms and diverse ways. It is a
like combination of filaments, lines, veins, passages, or the like:

There are many types of ways to network which consists of the following:

Radio and Television. a group of transmitting stations linked
by wire or microwave.

Relay so that the same program can be broadcasted or telecast by all.
A company or organization that provides
programs to be broadcast over these stations

Telecommunications:

Computers a system
containing any combination of computers,

computer terminals, printers, audio or v
isual
display devices, or telephones interconn
ected by
telecommunication equipment or cables
: used to
transmit or receive information.

An association of individuals having a c
ommon
interest, formed to provide mutual assis
tance, helpful information, or the like:

A
system of interrelated buildings, offices,
stations, etc., especially over a large ar
ea or throughout a country, territory, or
region.

Electricity:
An arrangement of conducting
elements, as resistors, capacitors, or in
ductors, connected by conducting wire.

To cultivate people who can be helpful t
o oneprofessionally,
especially in finding employ
mentor moving to a higher
 position.

To place (as a program from a local rad
io ortelevision station) in or on a netwo
rk:

To connect to a network.

To distribute widely:

To cover with or as if with a network:

To organize into a network:

To broadcast (a program) over a radio
or television network.

We will remain on business networking. Starting a business can be hard work. The entrepreneur or Ceo is seeking for tools and resources to build their brand of business.

You don't where to start or who to connect with. I can reflect back when we started our first non profit business. I was launched into the deep with nothing. I didn't have any audience, no tools, no resources, and no money.

So the first thing I thought about was to begin giving back. I started in a community center in Memphis, Tennessee. I was trying to target the "white collar" colleagues. Not knowing that I was not ready for that type of audience yet.

My first event was planning, preparation, finances, refreshments, planning for my mission and vision of the business, and more. There were so many things to consider in a brief period of time.

I had to rewind and consider some things first. I went online to search for webinars regarding to event planning and venues. I watched them over and over until I reached the level where I needed to be.

I rescheduled the event and it was a tremendous success. Online webinars and radio podcasts are easy and costless ways of training yourself how to run your business.

Many women whom I interview on the show have mentors and paid coaches. But I was starting from scratch. I had to utilize self training tools 🔨 in order to brand my business.

The more I planned and created events, this allowed me and my team to meet some very professional and profiled business owners and entrepreneurs.

The more I planned and organized the planning of the events became easier.

It began to work smoother and smoother.

How to Network

Did you know this was bottle-neck for me in the beginning? I didn't have any skills or training of how to network at any networking events. I wasn't invited to any network groups from anyone. I was just out there.

I attended an event about two years ago and the first thing I did was go to the refreshments section. I though the networking opportunity wasn't going to be that long. I thought I would go ahead and get me a small bite.

As I was preparing to sit down; a small group of people approached me and began asking who I was and began introducing themselves. IU thought ugh!

I knew that I had made a wrong move of going to get refreshments first. So I played it off by grabbing my business cards and stood up and began collaborating. What an embarrassing moment!

After that day; I began to become the networking expert. I wanted to know and learn everything I could of how to present myself at a networking event and know what not to do

I think we all can share some stories of how we didn't have it quite together the first time.

We had an opportunity to introduce ourselves and mention our business and brief mission. I didn't have any training on this either. But I knew and felt I had this down packed. Why? They all applauded after I made my verbal presentation.

Now I wasn't feeling so awkward now. I knew I was in the right room at the right time. There will many errors which we all make. We need to record them, learn from them, and move on.

Purpose of Networking

Before attending an event either by registering or invite; you must find your purpose for attending. Have you been to events, luncheons, conferences, or seminars; and you felt out of place?

Knowing your purpose for attending a networking event is essential. Sometimes attendees exit the venue with a sense of "wasted energy."

They will attend these events without a motive or purpose. I was invited to a free luncheon . It was a major bank conference. There were enough dignitaries there to fill up a gymnasium.

I was ready to go with my business cards. I enjoyed the huge conference, but I wasn't focused on the event. My business wasn't in banking or finances. But I did receive an opportunity to meet some interesting people.

With attending any event, you want to make sure that you are maximizing your time in the event. If all you are doing is sitting like "Plain Jane" at the seating area; you have not found your purpose for attending the event.

There were many types of targets there. There were audiences for religion, entrepreneurs, bankers, hotel staff, clergy, and more.

One of our nonprofits is coaching women. So my focus would to attend a networking event in regards to women. We have another nonprofit which hosts trade shows and expos. I would need to attend a networking event which consists of large conferences or event planning.

Knowing your purpose for attending will allow you to retrieve great results from your networking. Many businesses and entrepreneurs plan online networking. We plan online networking as well, but to get the full benefits from your business you would need to meet and greet face-to-face with your clients.

This is one of our strategies in a Metropolitan area. We host monthly event to network with other businesses, entrepreneurs, entry level start up businesses, and more.

Every business should be tangible for those in nearby communities and cities to get to know you and your business better.

This is an excellent way to brand your business and to be more tangible to gain more clientele.

Clients are interested in your products to be presented on the front line not on internet.

Once you've found your purpose for networking; you can begin to build your network and email subscribers list.

You will know that you have achieved your goal and purpose. There will be a sense of satisfaction which comes over you.

I can reflect back on about four years ago being asked to partner with a business. I just knew that I was on my way to stardom. No! Wait! Not so fast!

The business was more interested in finding ways to gain more than just to network. I planned my first event in partnership with them. The results were not good at all. The senior partner brought staff with him which was there to record how I was setting up the venue and the seminar.

I was outraged. I had driven an hour or so to meet up with this company and they tried to get their efforts managed first. A few minutes after the seminar; our partnership was severed. I terminated the relationship with a written contract and learned my lesson to move on further.

Making sure that you do your homework about businesses and companies can save you some hardship down the road. They were interested in partnering to drive my clients to their business for educational credits and career.

A paid expense was involved. Once I did a little research further; the business had lost some credibility in the area which we were both servicing.

They were not interested in networking. They were trying to use our business to build their credibility back.

I contacted them and confronted them of their actions. Of course, they were acting as if they were surprised. But I continued to fire back at

them and terminate their partnership.

It is very important to know beforehand whom you are networking with.

If you have received business cards from other networker; go online after the event to search the business owner or entrepreneur out.

It is healthy to make wise choices of your partners.

The Right Venue

If you are an event planner or attend live events; the venue is a key as well in networking.

I have planned over 100 events since 2011. So you see I plan a lot of events. In the beginning, I planned them to be

less cost effective.

But this will not build your business. You cannot build a business or company with venues which aren't compatible to your business.

As I stated before; I went to the community centers in the area. While this was okay, they weren't my target audience. So what I did; I started from the ground up.

I learned how to serve first with those in the community centers (low cost venues). This was my networking phase.

I began to grow in many ways and continue to meet other professionals whom were learning of my business. Once I achieved this level, I graduated so to speak from those areas into the target audience which I desired to have.

I went from low cost or no cost venues to paid venues. This was my training phase. I learned how to serve others first. This will grow you and your business as an expert.

I feel that no business owner can be successful unless they know how to serve first.

Some paid venues have more amenities to offer than those which are free and of low cost.

When networking or planning networking events; you want to make sure that the venue is suitable for your attendants.

The first Health Fair I hosted gained more complaints which caused me to move the future events at other locations. When planning events; you will need a checklist for your venues.

Making sure that the director of your venue is held to high standards when booking venues; is very important.

Clean and professional venues; is part of your business card ![clapperboard] . It exemplifies of who you are and what sort of taste you acquire.

Attendants will not be interested in your networking event if your venue is not professional and well selected.

Results and Follow up of Networking

We all have been guilty of this. We have attended a networking event and forgot about the business cards which we have retrieved.

I have so many business cards here in the office that I cannot count them and become tired. We should have a plan to follow up with those whom we have retrieved the business cards from.

What is the purpose of asking networking attendants for their business cards; and you aren't going to utilize them.

I know that you feel that some don't want you to contact them. But this is the purpose. You also can send them an email after the event and ask them if you could edit them into your newsletters or email database.

Some will not allow you to contact them after the event. Why? Some professionals are complete with the event after they attend. If they have met more clients and potential leads for business; then they feel they have enough.

The Right Target Audience & Connections

Social Media platforms are a huge plus for business. It allows entrepreneurs and business owners to connect and network online.

You can reach a broader audience over these platforms. I can remember when I first signed up for these platforms; I was all over the place. I had everyone in the same group, feed, and timeline.

I was confused as to why anyone was connecting with me. Once I learned more about whom I desired to target; then everything made sense.

I went back and managed my groups, my accounts, and pages. I deleted the platforms and restarted my accounts. Your audience or clients may become easily confused by what and who is on your feed.

This is why it is important whom you are friends with on social media. I try to make sure that I read their about page and whom they represent.

If they aren't in business, career advancements, or business owner; I will not accept their friend request.

People such as your clients and audience will view you according to whom you are connected with. Sometimes I will take the opportunity to view the requester's friends as well. You remember the old saying; "Birds of a feather flock together."

We want to make sure that we are reaching them. Social media shouldn't take up all of the time in the day.

Our business should be flourishing in diverse ways so that social media isn't our main networking source.

Training yourself with networking literature in your spare of leisure time is a healthy source for growth in business as well.

Your Business Card

What is your business card? It is information printed on a display for others to view about you.

Well, we are going to go a little deeper. Your business card is also how you represent yourself.

This consists of your attire, your venue, your representation, your speakers and more. Your business card is your mission and vision statement. If you aren't aware already what this is; there is no need to attend the networking event. The first thing that you will be asked is; "What do you do"?

The next thing you will be asked is; Do you have a business card with you?" You must be prepared in a 360° format. You must be fully loaded and prepared.

Summary

You can succeed in anything once you have the major keys in place. Networking allows the entrepreneur to connect and collaborate with professionals on a face to face manner.

Entrepreneurs can get more from networking at live events than online. Making sure that you have enough tools and resources handy at your networking event can land points for your business.

Always be selective and spontaneous when planning or attending an event. Now get out there and GO Networking!

About The Author

Diane is a native of Pontiac, Michigan. She is an author, publisher- editor, speaker, radio show host, event planner, and blogger. Diane is the chief Empowerment officer of the National Extraordinary Professional Women and Chief Executive officer of the Networking Partners.

She has over 25 years of leadership skills and development. Her objective goals are to provide training skills and resources for entrepreneurs and business owners to enhance their business.